Paris.
Its artistic h
Haussman's boulevards, s
historic bridges, and popu
museums. But this legacy can become a millstone
when the city is also expected to tread the cutting edge of art. Paris has often been criticised
for relying too much on its past. Still, after
a hiatus during the 1980–90s, a brand new Paris
is starting to shine: ripe with fresh takes on
fashion, food and modern art.

This renaissance is most obvious in the culinary
scene where the starched white tablecloths of
Michelin-starred restaurants are whipped aside
in favour of a local, uncomplicated cuisine based
on quality ingredients. Meanwhile, a magnetic
fashion scene shows there's enough room alongside major houses for a multitude of free-
thinking creators.

Because in the end, it's the people who make the
place. In Paris, we spoke to a minted fashion
legend, a creative couple about their well-trodden
paths and a design curator with an eye for beauty.
Which is something the French capital has in
spades—making it an ideal city to get lost in.

8

29   JUILLET   1881

One can definitely not summarize Paris to a list of restaurants, cafés and landmarks because Paris, in the words of legendary architecture critic Ian Nairn "is urging you to greater depth of feeling" by observing the finely grained details the city offers. From the serifs in the 19th century typograhpy to the poetry in the subway names such as Sèvres-Babylone, it is in the streets that one can admire the hidden elegance the city has to offer. On rue du Bac or rue de l'Échaudé one can admire Haussmanian architecture and

unexpected views on great monuments such as the Church of Saint Sulpice, Servandoni's masterpiece. On the right bank, onc can stumble upon hidden alleys, Rue des Thermopyles in the 14th or Cité Pilleux in the 18th, spaces in the interstices of the squares and boulevards which make the city a collective masterpiece.
• Various locations

Jaw-dropping. That's just one way to describe this former *Communist Party headquarters*. Designed by Oscar Niemeyer for an idyllic tomorrow, the two-part structure boasts the timeless lines and ratios of an undying Modernist sensibility. In fact, the building itself has outlasted the communists—the last of whom have been relegated to a corner office somewhere upstairs. The centre's auditorium and an art exhibit are open to all those willing to venture outside the city.

• Siège du parti communiste Français, 2 place du Colonel-Fabien, 19th arr. espace-niemeyer.fr

From Art-filled Parks to Historical Bars

Paris S'éveille

Leisure | Brough to Heel

This much-needed green lung sits between Saint-Germain-des-Pres and the Latin Quarter. Rent a toy boat, sit down for a chess match, stroll around and take in the sculptures, the Medici fountain, greenhouses or English-style gardens. Or make like the Parisians and pick up a basket of cheese, meats and wine to splay out on the delightfully-manicured lawns. An activity which can be conveniently combined with soaking up the sun and doing some of the city's finest people watching. The lovely green oasis is a charming way to while away a summer afternoon.

• Jardin du Luxembourg, 6th arr.

Shop | Attention, Shoppers

The "trendiest store in the world" is but a sweet memory, and there is yet to appear another retail champion to step up and carry the torch. Merci does a good job in the homewares arena, but if you ask any fashion-minded Parisian worth their salt where they would take you for a good dose of design, they'll say *Le Bon Marché*. Housed in a structure that dates back to 1838 and is an architectural draw unto itself, the store's decorators go all-out to provide a positively festive experience—no matter the time of year. Paris' most beloved department store offers a stellar selection of both classic and emerging brands in everything from food to decor to clothing. You'll also encounter the mandatory sighting of the local Hermes-scarved bourgeoisie—tiny dogs and all. Make like the ladies and lunch along with them in the fantastic in-house epicerie.

• Le Bon Marché, 24 Rue de Sèvres, 7th arr. 24sevres.com

Driven by Design

Located in the 1st near the Louvre, the *Musée des Arts Decoratifs* originated in 1882, in the wake of the Universal Exhibitions, when a group of collectors banded together with the idea of promoting the applied arts and developing links between industry and culture, design and production. Today one can find exhibits around fashion, architecture and design and an impressive permanent collection which displays products from the Middle Ages to today.
• Musée des Arts Décoratifs,
107 Rue de Rivoli, 1st arr.
madparis.fr

The Grinning Cat

Look close enough and you'll notice a certain entertained feline marking his territory across all of Paris. Thoma Vuille's Monsieur Chat, the grinning cat, could be considered a cross between Charles Schultz's innocent humour and Spiderman, risking his neck to put a smile on the denizens of Paris. The cat was immortalised by Chris Marker's documentary The Case of the Grinning Cat, in which he uses the phenomenon of the yellow cat's appearance as a chance to reflect on the state of the country.
• Various locations

10

Food | Old Faithful

Au Pied de Cochon could not be more Parisian if it tried. From checkered tablecloths to red curving lampshades to the endless parade of pig prepared every which way, this is not so much a tourist trap as it is a glorious, still-relevant ode to the undying spirit of the French capital. Open 24 hours, seven days a week since it's inauguration in 1946, the brasserie and its entire menu are a more than a safe bet for those yearning for dinner at four in the morning—whatever the reason.
• Au Pied de Cochon, 6 Rue Coquillière, pieddecochon.com

Shop | Old World Delight

There are certain things you can count on in Paris—and striking gold on rue Saint Honoré is one of them. Following the tradition of 18th-century ceramic studios, *Astier de Villate* makes refined china and ceramics in keeping with bygone style, albeit with a modern twist. Find the obligatory platesalongside scented candles and limited-edition lines made in collaboration. A stone's throw away you'll find *Diptyque*, whose pop-up turned permanent home offers shoppers not only a superb olfactory experience, but a visual one as well.
• Various locations

Cosima Ungaro & Austin Feilders
She grew up half French, half
Italian. He also split his upbringing
between American English and
French. Together, they run Concept,
a creative studio that decants the
duo's worldly experience into ser-
vices for art, hospitality and luxury
brands

Cosima Ungaro & Austin Feilders, Brand and Creative Directors

Blazing Trails

What do a French-Italian fashion darling and an American in Paris
have in common? Besides holy matrimony and their creative agency,
Austin and Cosima know the lay of their land. From where to stock
up for a good house party to who makes noodles worth crossing the
river for, their Paris is one of spoils and delicacies

*You live in the 6th arrondissement,
describe your neighborhood for us.
Is it your favorite area of the city?*

Cosima: We both grew up on the
left bank, just a few streets apart
in the 7th arrondissement. We spent
the last ten years travelling, study-
ing and working all over the world.
Austin lived in Buenos Aires, Cape
Town, California and West Africa
for a time, while I lived in Barcelona
and London. We just moved back
from New York a few years ago.
There's no place like Paris.

Austin: We went to the same high
school in Paris, same university in
Montreal, but ended up meeting at
an airport.

Now we live right across from
the Luxembourg gardens. We call
the left bank home.

Cosima: We ride to the right
bank for dinner at *Vivant* in the
10th, we are big on Japanese food
at *Kunitoraya*, *Echizen Soba Togo*
or *Abri Soba*. The list is endless.
But we love crossing back over the
bridge to the peacefulness of the
left bank.

Austin: It's our Brooklyn to the
right bank's feeling of Manhattan.
The quiet streets, squares like Place
Saint Sulpice and cafés like the
Flore remind us of the Brasserie Les
Deux Garçons and strolling along
the Cours Mirabeau in Aix en
Provence. Cosi and I both grew up
partly in the South of France. My
parents used to have a house in the
Luberon and Cosi still has a family
home called La Cavalerie where
we produce small batches of organic
olive oil for friends and family.

*Some locations to look out for on
the left bank?*

Look for Rimbaud's poem Le
Bateau Ivre on the wall of rue
Férou. Close by you'll find *Le Bon
Saint Pourcain*. For the baba au
rhum, the poularde; three entrees,
three mains, perfect every time.

For travel journals, sketchbooks,
incredible paper and art supplies,
stop by *Sennelier*, a 19th-century
boutique on the quai Voltaire.
Sagan is a very discreet Japanese
restaurant by the Theatre de
l'Odeon. For Soba, head to *Yen* by
Saint Germain-des-Pres. Then
there's the *Alain Ducasse* chocolate
store tucked away behind the
Flore on rue Saint Benoit, he just
opened a coffee place on rue du
Cherche Midi as well. *Ceccaldi* is
a traditional Corsican knife maker
on rue Racine. And you can get
your coffee at *Coutume* on rue de
Babylone, at *Circus* on rue Galande,
or *Shakespeare and Company* on
the quai de Montebello. Our tailor,
Noel Dorado, is on the corner of
rue de Babylone and rue Vaneau.
He consults for Virgil Abloh,
designs costumes for Lady Gaga
and arranges parade uniforms for
officers of the French republican
guard.

*Cosima, you have been immersed in
the art and fashion worlds from
a very early age. How do you see the
fashion landscape evolving in Paris?*

Cosima: I have a very vivid
memory of my parents working in
the fashion world at the height
of my father's couture house in the
nineties. In those years, fashion
revolved around much fewer
designers, who were couturiers in
the real sense of the term: Saint
Laurent, Alaïa, Lacroix, Galliano...
Today, the people at the helm of
the major houses are very strong
creative directors but I believe it's
not quite the same métier, nor the
same creative process. I remember
taking a slow boat through Laos
with my family crossing the Mekong
river, my father was writing the
whole way. As we stepped off the
boat he looked at us and said he
had the next collection ready. The
clothes he made sparked from his

Racines, the trattoria from Sardinian wild child Simone Tondo, serves Italian fare and boasts a Michelin star

dreams. I am not sure anyone works like that today. To quote Cathy Horyn: "Where is the Kawakubo of today, or the Margiela? or Helmut Lang? Where are those people who can really make a statement about their times?"

Austin, as an American living in Paris—apart from the Thomas Jefferson statue and the Paris Review, do you see any interesting links remaining between the US and Paris?
     Austin: "This is not McDonald's". That's what the waiters at the Flore will tell you. So come by ship if you have to, bring along your American enthusiasm and creativity, but leave the rest of your baggage behind. This is Paris, there's nothing like it!

Cosima, can you say anything about Italians and their connection to Paris. Any Italian restaurants here worth the detour?
     Racines just received a Michelin

star. The young chef, Simone Tondo is all about fantastic produce. *Passerini* is also one of our favourites. Rue Saint Maur has a tiny shop called *Cooperativa Latte Cisternino*, which has been the main supplier for the parties we host.

Tell us what a perfect Sunday in Paris looks like.
     Cosima: Austin goes running in the park or by the river. I bike down the street to go for a swim. We meet for a stroll at the organic market on boulevard Raspail to grab a roast chicken, some fresh vegetables and gather friends at home for a long and lazy lunch around the fireplace in the winter and out on our terrace in the summer.

If there's time to go away for the day or one night just outside of town —where to?
     Cosima: It's not right outside of Paris, but definitely worth a trip:

Chalet 1864 in the Grand Bornand, French Alps.

Austin: My brother, who first launched seven years ago, which to me is the best organic burger in Paris, just renovated a 19th-century seven bedroom estate that you can rent by the Seine just outside of Paris called *Riverside House Normandy.*

Where did you find your last vintage treasure?

Cosima: Tokyo! In Paris, I would highly recommend the flea market at the Portes de Vanves, which has more unexpected finds than the Puces de Clignancourt in my opinion.

Who makes breakfast worth waking up for?

Cosima: *Mokonuts* during the week, especially when breakfast turns into lunch. *Dersou* on the weekends.

Favorite bakery.

Cosima: *Circus bakery* for their sourdough bread and cinnamon rolls. Unfortunately only opens from Thursday to Monday.

Austin: *Tomo* for warm wajima salt red bean dorayaki on the right bank.

Favorite terrace.

Cosima: *Le Nemours* at golden hour.

A spot in the city that never ceases to inspire?

Austin: Biking along the quai de Bourbon and quai d'Orleans on the Ile Saint Louis reminds us of being on the canals in Amsterdam.

Where do you wish you went more often?

Cosima: Rome for a cappuccino at Roscioli Café! In Paris, probably the *Louvre*, often very wrongly overlooked by locals.

Where do you get your cultural fix in the city?

Cosima: Paris is impressive in terms of cultural offering and we take advantage of it all. We try never to miss an exhibit, especially the ones taking place at the *Jeu de Paume, Fondation Cartier* and *Musée Maillol.*

Perfect soundtrack for your city?

Austin: J.S. Ondara's "Revolution Blues". He just played at *Point Ephemere* by the Canal. Ondara is a US-based Nairobi-born singer songwriter who grew up listening to Bob Dylan and Neil Young. A reminder that we can still combine national identity with a global ethos.

Le Nemours is a Right Bank insititution where you can sip coffee alongside actors and local politicians

South Pigalle & Canal Saint-Martin
Parisian Pulse

Two northern areas jostling to be the hip heart of new Paris: SoPi, or South of Pigalle, has swapped call girls for cool cats, while fresh foods, drinks and arts are lining Canal Saint-Martin

Food | Close Encounter

Darling chef Iñaki Aizpitarte has all but made *Le Chateaubriand* a foodie household name thanks to a modern, prix fixe offering and a selection of new world wines. But if you're short on time and a reservation isn't in the books (or you've checked it off and want to try more), keep things simple and pop in next door to *Le Dauphin*. Its sister joint may be smaller and require less fanfare, but the level of quality remains—both are helmed by the same overachiever. Decked out in a Rem Koolhaas-designed marble interior, this one's all about smaller plates and natural wines. From perfectly-executed seafood like the unbeatable sole meunière, crab or goos barnacles to the straight-up superb ham and chorizo. For lunch, it's a slimmer and more affordable menu of Asian-inspired soups and a daily dessert. Come for both meals—nobody will blame you.
• Le Dauphin, 131 avenue Parmentier, restaurantledauphin.net

Liberty or Croissants

The concept behind Liberté was to take down the walls between kitchen and counter in order to demystify and "free" the baking process. The open kitchen view allows customers to admire the confection process of all the different pastries, while the massive marble counter sets a clean stage for the assortment of creations. Purists and the more adventurous will find delight in the mandatory classics, displayed alongside inventive treats like glazed strawberry croissants or lemon choud with a newfangled spin on it.
• Patisserie Liberté, 39 Rue des Vinaigriers, 10th arr. libertepatisserieboulangerie.com

Bordello Be Gone

Hôtel Amour isn't your typical hotel—and its restaurant isn't your typical hotel eatery either. On a busy side street in the So-Pi area, this former bordello has been completely transformed by nightlife moguls Thierry Costes and André Saraiva. The restaurant serves straightforward French dishes and is always buzzing. Try to get a table in their beautiful courtyard—it's a little tropical paradise in the middle of the city, complete with palm trees and a koi pond. They also do one of the best brunches in town.
• Hôtel Amour, 8 Rue de Navarin, 9th arr., hotelamourparis.fr

Dress Code: Conscious

Set up by the two founders of ubiquitous eco-sneaker brand Veja, Centre Commercial is a menswear store nestled just off of the Canal Saint-Martin. In keeping with the area's café-lined streets and slow pace, the boutique offers a gentle mix of smart, tailored separates for men as well as a curation of books, organic cosmetics, vintage furniture and restored bicycles. Yes, there's also something for the ladies and yes, the entire selection is a perfect amalgam of the pair's worldly influences—making for an utterly pleasant shopping experience.
• Centre Commercial, 2 Rue de Marseille, 10th arr. centrecommercial.cc

Some trips
for bad

re too short
meals.

Make sure they're
all good with the LOST iN app.

From Where We Stand

It was 2012 when I walked through Colette's doors for the very first time. Though I recognised the façade immediately, the Givaudan-designed scent of ripe figs was the first thing to catch me by surprise. All those articles, photos and posts had not fully prepared me for an encounter that had been a long time coming.

For years the digital murmur of a Parisian mecca of cool had been growing louder and louder, the waves finally reaching my screen way down in South America. So much so that when it came time to move to Europe, Colette was among the many things that might finally get checked off the fashion bucket list. It was the season of Christopher Kane's 3D flower appliqués —a searing hot marker of hip which the Rue Saint Honoré boutique obviously had on display, and which turned out to be even prettier in person than on screen. The off-the-runway looks shared racks with Star Wars merch and skate decks. There was a Kenny Scharf show going on upstairs with limited-edition collectibles for sale. That first visit lasted a full three hours.

Hype is a tricky thing. In fashion, where trends are pronounced dead before they really catch on and the search for the next great thing is never ending, the mere endowment of "cool" usually signifies something's demise. And so, for silhouettes, brands, shops and even colour palettes to live up to and survive the over indexing and over-digestion is a special feat indeed. For Colette, the OG cool kid, there has been no hype too exaggerated.

Colette opened its doors on Rue Saint Honoré in 1997 to a very different world. It was seven years before Facebook was even created, and a whopping thirteen before the existence of Instagram. Britney was on the cusp of her career and denim on denim on denim was about the coolest thing you could step outside wearing. It was a time before hashtags, "shop now" features and the ubiquitous use of the term "disruptor". And yet disrupt is exactly what this, perhaps the world's first serious concept store, did to the global retail landscape. Velour tracksuits went out of fashion, Chandelier earrings came in. Trucker hats gave way to the age of the stiletto and then Phoebe Philo turned everyone into a minimalist. Our brand-new feeds were inundated with inspiration and aspiration as some brands started to become experts at branding themselves. But Colette had been good at that since the beginning. Take the popularity of its trademark Pantone 293c—the shade of its logo and countless limited-edition collaboration products—as just one sign.

The kind of high-low fashion edits concept shops have become known for were practically unheard of 20 years ago. Inspired by their travels and the space on Saint Honoré at their disposal, Colette Rousseaux and daughter Sarah Andelman decided to channel a vision for bringing all their favourite things together. For Andelman—a tireless aesthete with a nose for what's good—, this meant a refreshing mix of high fashion, trending sneakers, edgy streetwear and the kind of small-run

"They have invented a formula that you can't copy easily, because there is only one Colette and her and Sarah are 200 percent involved", said Karl Lagerfeld of the late concept store

collections by designers whose careers she helped launch. They include the now-ubiquitous Proenza Schouler, Simone Rocha and Rodarte. A café and robust inventory of lifestyle products like books and homewares turned the place into a one-stop shop. You could walk out of Colette as a better version of yourself.

One of the names on the list of fledgling designers favoured by Rousseauxn and Andelman was Esteban Cortázar's. As part of the "Colombia-France Year", a cultural initiative to foster ties between the countries, the Miami-raised designer turned Colette into a full-blown Colombian kiosk complete with typical sweets and limited-edition products by Cortázar and friends, made specially for the occasion. The pop-up, held during the store's bittersweet last couple of months, would receive support from the Colombian embassy in a demonstration of just how far Colette came in establishing itself as a serious cultural contender.

It's this multidimensional aspect that also served to cement its reputation—going far beyond mere concept store to become a cultural hub. From panel discussions about sneaker culture to live shows and book signings, the 740 square metre space was a testament to Andelman and Rousseaux's perennial quest to keep things exciting.

Many have marvelled at the shop's knack for getting it right, turning a 20-year trajectory into an upward curve. If allowed a theory on this, I might posit that their secret has lied in simple humility. Perhaps not rare but certainly special in the world of fashion, it was Colette's ability to stay humble that allowed it to focus on what truly mattered—finding and filling the shop with wonderful additions to anyone's life. An ethos for kindness in dealing with any brand, be it Saint Laurent or this humble travel guide, should serve as an obvious yet seldom-followed example for those running any kind of business. Along with the no-bull-shit barometer that let it survive through wave after wave of self-imploding hype, it's almost thrilling to realise that Colette's constant quest to look different, renew and discover was never to appease any audience or critic, but rather the mission of its founders to outdo only themselves. Over and over. True to the twenty-year fashion life cycle, the pendulum eventually swung back to a place very similar to where it was when Colette began its journey. From Dr. Martens to Yeezy, Vespa to BUSCEMI and Apple, the list of the brand's eager collaborators reads like a what's what of 21st century consumerism. Velvet was in vogue, as were dainty chokers and barely-there slip dresses. The 1990s aesthetic came roaring back to life—except at this point we would buy into it through our Instagram feeds. For Colette's 870K followers, those feeds lost just a little magic on December 20, 2017.

In line with its commitment to keeping things classy, Colette turned down the expected barrage of offers to purchase the brand, deciding instead to switch the lights off on its own terms. For the countless concept stores that have opened since 1997 and will continue to carry the torch, the key to success might lie beyond the marketing strategies and in something much more human. Perhaps, simply an attitude. When asked about the moment they realised they'd created something special, Andelman's answer was succinct: "We never did".

Anja Simona is a Caracas-born, Miami-raised Uruguayan writer and editor based in Berlin. For café reviews and wiener dogs, @anja_simona.

Martine de Menthon
She's a freelance stylist who has
worked in fashion for four decades,
with names like Guy Bourdin,
Helmut Newton, Chanel, Vogue
and Egoisten

Martine de Menthon, Stylist

Bona Fide

Martine is a fashion industry legend. From assisting the editor in
chief of French Vogue to styling all the big names wearing the even
bigger names, this through-and-through Parisian takes stock of
her city and career with the excitement and nonchalance of some-
one who's seen it all—and still loves it

As a stylist yourself, is there such a thing as "the" Parisian style?

All the big names in fashion were either themselves Parisian or came to Paris in order to receive their crown. Even for Italians such as Valentino, Paris is still their stage. The birthplace of Haute Couture, the first place of pret-a-porter. Fashion is now global, but Paris is still where talents come for their validation. You get your crown in Paris.

Can you talk to us about great shows?

Saint Laurent of course, at Avenue Marceau. Galliano for Dior at Bagatelle or at the Gare de Lyon where he would stage cowboys and indians. Gianni Versace at the Ritz pool. Valentino just did a stunning show at the Hotel Salomon de Rothschild.

Where would one go to get a feel for current Paris fashion?

A few months ago I would have said Colette. Unfortunately, since Colette's closing, we have all been waiting for a multi-brand store to come in and take its place. Sarah and Colette were both pioneers with a real vision beyond just buying. Nonetheless, Le Bon Marché remains a good store to get a feel for the scene.

With the emergence of streetwear taking its place among the big fashion houses today, can we still speak of haute couture?

The niche of haute couture is actually seeing a resurgence. All thanks to talented creative directors such as Pierpaolo Picciolo at Valentino, which does real, well-researched, extremely refined haute couture. Dior, Givenchy and Chanel's ateliers are also keeping the craft alive thanks to a highly skilled set of artisans and brodeurs; there's a lot of know-how.

Where to shop for fashion in Paris?

I am lucky to live in the 7th, in the heart of a fashion district. Thanks to the *Bon Marché* you have an interesting corner between Prada and Celine, but you can also find emerging brands such as Ami, which I like very much. Avenue Montaigne is mostly for the buyers from abroad, but one can definitely catch a glimpse of all the brands that are relevant in high fashion today. Faubourg Saint Honoré, meanwhile, caters to more people and remains one of the most important streets for fashion.

Any Parisian figures you can tell us about?

I was very close to Azzedine Alaïa, he was first a great friend. Through an extraordinary sequence of events he met the writer Louise de Vilmorin and started working at Dior as a "petite main" but got ejected once the war in Algeria broke out. He became the couturier to Vilmorin and dressed Greta Garbo and lived in a small apartment on rue de Bellechasse, where he stored fantastic dresses in the bathroom. We still feel his influence throughout the city and in his headquarters at 18 rue de la Verrerie in the 8th. The place, which is open to visitors, has a large glass ceiling under which were his apartment, his atelier, his office and his shop. Interesting fact, the building used to house Madame de Pompadour, Louis XV's main mistress. Azzedine came out with a collection which was very much inspired by the 18th century without knowing that the Madame who used to give so much importance to clothing had graced the same location. Un grand monsieur. Meanwhile, the photographer that impressed me the most was Guy Bourdin. He started off as a salesman at BHV and then met

Despite its tourist attraction status, "the Flore" remains a gathering point for locals

Ami
7th arr.

Man Ray, which set him off. A man with an infinite imagination. He would call me up in the morning asking for a glass sarcophagus, a studio filled with baby chicks or a lamb's head. You can imagine what it smelled like in there after three days.

The glossy magazine is still one of the world's windows into fashion. Can you tell us about your experience with publications?

At french Vogue I was assistant editor in chief. I then created my styling agency, where I did Chanel advertisements and editorials for Egoiste magazine. As for what I consume, I go to *WH Smith* on rue de Rivoli to get my fix.

Paris as a backdrop for a shoot never gets old... Any locations that continue to inspire you?

So many. We've used the famous corner Helmut Newton shot on rue Aubriot multiple times. The Opera, where I have a great souvenir of Baryshnikov jumping down the stairs, putting his ankle at risk. Theatres and gardens like the Tuileries or Bagatelle.

Any location in Paris which should be used for a fashion show?

After 40 years in the industry between pret-a-porter and haute couture, I can honestly say that the location scouts have already combed through every little corner and dead end street. We've seen it all.

Young french designers to be excited about?

Alexandre Mattiussi at Ami, which is an up-and-coming brand. Pallas is contemporary but with a classical base. Marine Serre is very entertaining. Julien Dossena at Paco Rabanne is one to keep an eye on.

Beauty is also synonymous with Paris. Any brands to watch out for?
   Buly, a project by Victoire de Taillac and Ramdane Touhami takes a modern approach to a very old look, along the lines of Astier de Villate. *Diptyque* in Saint Germain has products I like very much. For skincare, I would say *Joëlle Ciocco*.

Favorite place to have a glass of champagne and do some people watching?
   Café de Flore, I have been coming here since forever. I always sit inside. The locals always sit inside. Except for one person, the legendary photographer Jeanloup Sieff, a photographer with a hitchcockian style who is famous for his Yves Saint Laurent portrait. Every morning he would have breakfast here on the terrace at his spot in the the corner.

As for culture, any favourite museums or galleries?
   Fondation Louis Vuitton, which has a great programme. I always enjoy going to *The Musée de la Chasse* and *Galerie Kamel Mennour*.

A historical location in Paris that no longer exists?
   7 Rue Saint-Anne was The Sept, which later became The Palace. Owner Fabrice Emaer was very close, he'd invite a group every week on Wednesday. If Warhol was in town he was there. A refined decadence.

Three Parisians dead or alive which you would like to have dinner with and where.
   Author Romain Gary at the *Le Bar des Près sushi bar*, actress Arletty at *Le Bristol* and the larger than life Gerard Depardieu I would take to the tiny restaurant *Cibus*.

Officine Universelle Buly, home to a revived beauty brand, offers perfumes, atmospheric scents and beauty treatments

Art Concret

A showcase by Alexandre Tabaste

Thanks to his formal training as an architect, Alexandre Tabaste got his start in photography through capturing buildings. As his career evolved, the human figure gained prominence in his work by way of an interest in fashion photography. Through the juxtaposition of these two worlds we bear witness to the duality and complementarity of the human and the structural.

French Revolution

David Jenal

In November 1962, Ileana Sonnabend opened an exhibition space on 37, quai des Grands-Augustins, on the bank of the river Seine, with a show of paintings by Jasper Johns.

At that time, the American artist was already a celebrated figure in New York and throughout the US, but far less known in Europe. Thus, Sonnabend's choice for her debut in Paris wasn't without risk. Looking back, it paid off: today, Jasper Johns is considered one of the most important artists of the 20th century, with his works being part of the collections of major museums and private collectors in the US, Europe and beyond.

The gallery Ileana Sonnabend established that winter shaped the art scene of Paris like little else throughout the twentieth century. And what's more, the art dealer was a driving power in introducing US-American artists to the European public, an endeavour that culminated in Robert Rauschenberg winning the grand prize at the Venice Biennale in 1964. The fact that Sonnabend, who simultaneously ran a gallery space in New York, decided for Paris as for her European dependence, comes at no surprise considering the city's rich and churning history of art dealing (the latter due to one revolution and two world wars).

Towards the midst of the eighteenth century, French art dealer Edmé-François Gersaint was the first to publish auction elaborated catalogues, announcing upcoming art auctions to a broader audience. Subsequently, Paris became an art market epicenter, which only the French Revolution was able to bring down: French noble collections were seized in the course of the political and social upheaval, and market activities shifted towards London, where auction houses such as Christie's and Sotheby's emerged. However, the magic attraction of Paris to intellectuals and artists soon lead to a renewed flare-up of activity. Walter Benjamin called Paris "the capital of the nine-teenth century", and the rise of impressionist painters such as Monet, Degas and Renoir as well as Édouard Manet ringing in the modern period proved him right. Paris was on top of the world, and so was its art market: the city was amongst the first with a working system of independent, influential galleries, which did not rely heavily on official institutions and were con-stantly and observed by a critical specialist press.

Joseph Duveen, a legendary figure of the art market at the turn of the century, and just as flamboyant and crafty one could imagine an art dealer to be, realized the importance of Paris at an early stage of his career. He temporarily operated a gallery space in the city and unless did business in the Ritz hotel at Place Vendôme, where he acquired masterpieces from European noblemen, which he later sold to US-American industrials in New York at steep prices.

Duveen was succeeded by gallerists who perhaps operated their businesses in a more modest and discreet manner. Amongst them where René Gimpel and Daniel-Henry Kahnweiler, the former who was married to a sister of Duveen, the latter who grew up in Southern Germany and was amongst the first to pick up the works of Picasso. Kahnweiler opened his gallery in Paris 1907, simultaneously entering into exclusive contracts with artists such as Derain, Vlaminck and Braque. Only five years later, he started representing Pablo Picasso, to whom a friendship connected him henceforth. When World War I broke out, Kahnweiler wasn't in Paris, and his gallery including all stock was confiscated. In 1920 he returned to Paris and established a new gallery with the collaboration of André Simon. In the sequel, world history wasn't on his side: in the course of World War II, Kahnweiler had to flee from Paris to hide in Southern France due to his Jewish descent. The sister of his wife, who was in turn married to writer Michel Leiris, set forth the business of the gallery, which was naturally renamed to Galerie Louise Leiris. Kahnweiler returned to the gallery on the day of the end of the war.

US-American Leo Castelli, amongst the most influential figures of the art market in the twentieth century (and, on a side note, at that time married to Ileana Sonnabend), started his career as a gallerist in Paris, where he opened a gallery in 1939. However, the city was occupied by the Germans a year later and Castelli relocated to New York. It wasn't until the early 1960s, that the art market in Paris would accelerate again. In the prior decade, several artists and figures related to the creative industries moved from Paris to New York. As a logical consequence, Ileana Sonnabend opened up her gallery in the early 1960s, promoting US-American artists and investing in art that was considered difficult to sell in Europe. Sonnabend, also known as "mom of pop", referring to her continuous engagement for pop art, was the first to establish the Eastward direction for art to travel across the Atlantic. She made Paris the ground for iconic solo exhibitions with the likes of Robert Rauschenberg, Roy Lichtenstein, Andy Warhol, Mario Merz and Michelangelo Pistoletto. Her gallery masterly bridged Arte Povera and Pop Art over the course of several decades.

Today, Gagosian and Galerie Thaddaeus Ropac, two of the leading contemporary art galleries, run extensive exhibition spaces located in suburbs of Paris which provide room for large scale installations and over-dimensioned canvasses, in short art that doesn't fit the galleries' respective prime locations in Paris in the thriving neighbourhoods of Marais (Ropac) and Faubourg-du-Roule (Gagosian). Major galleries including Marian Goodman Gallery, Perrotin, Galerie Karsten Greve, kamel mennour and Air de Paris run dependences in Paris. Besides

Galerie Louise Leiris
47 Rue de Monceau
PARIS - 8e

PICASSO
dessins
1959-1960.
du 30 Novembre au 31 Decembre

Exhition poster for the Picasso show at Louise Leiris

Art mogul Leo Castelli invading the Parisian art scene.

them, emerging galleries such as Galerie Crèvecœur and Antoine Levi. In addition, every October the Grand Palais turns into a thriving market place for modern and contemporary art as it hosts the FIAC, one of the world's leading art fairs. The event gets sandwiched by smaller satellite fairs such as Paris Internationale, which showcase young and emerging galleries from all over the world.

David Jenal writes about contemporary art, the art market and pop culture. @ davidjenal

La Belle Vie

Shop · Food · Culture | **Tangled Streets**

Impressive classical monuments are scattered all over Paris, but it's in the Marais that most visitors lose their hearts to the city for the first time. This part of town started out as the aristocratic area—with city palaces and lavish residences—but when the royals moved away, the Jewish community of Paris settled in. Haut Marais, a tangle of tiny streets that runs from the Picasso Museum to the Place de la République, is an area made for exploring. With tons of galleries and amazing shops, it's very easy to spend hours here. Look out for *Merci* (pictured), the famous concept store that offers fashion for both men and women, great interior design products and luxurious skincare. Expect to run into some celebrities in the *Cinéma Café* next door, one of three eateries part of the shop. Smart French clothes are sold at *A.P.C.*, and luxe labels like *Isabel Marant* and *Acne* have also set up boutiques in the quarter too. For lunch, stop by *Nanashi* and partake of one of their bento boxes, or find yourself with a boeuf tartare on the terrace of *Café Charlot*. Later on, there is absolutely no better place for watching Parisians slink into the evening than *La Perle*. This bar and café is a favourite for the fashion and art crowd—they descend on it every night as soon as the showrooms in the neighbourhood close up. The wine here is inexpensive, delicious and sipped over conversations in many different languages.

• 3rd arr., various locations

Sparks of Sweden

Housed in a wonderful hôtel particulier, a private mansion from the 18th century, the *Swedish Institute in Paris* hosts exhibitions, film screenings and readings, and showcases young Swedish artists. The small café on the ground floor serves handmade smörgås (open-faced sandwiches with a variety of toppings) and, of course, kanelbullar (Swedish cinnamon rolls). In summer, the courtyard is a perfectly calm place to have a coffee and a pensive break.
• L'Institut Suédois à Paris, 11 rue Payenne, 3rd arr., paris.si.se

Food | **Electric Feel**

After cutting his teeth at Parisian eating institution Kitchen Galerie, local enfant prodige Adrien Ferrand decided to take its trademark refinement and precision to his own endeavour. The name-sake smoked eel comes highly recommended and is best partnered with any of the restaurant's natural or biodynamic wines.
• Eels, 27 Rue d'Hauteville, 10th arr., restaurant-eels.com

Shop | **Bobo Baggage**

FrenchTrotters is a Parisian brand slowly building a little empire in the city. Catering to the Bobo crowd (the young "bourgeois bohèmes" who often work in creative fields), their flagship store in the Rue Vieille du Temple stocks both their women's and men's collection and a small selection of other brands. Expect leather boots and denim jackets for the guys, understated blouses, leather jackets and corduroy skirts for the girls. There's current must-have printed matter on sale, plus a big selection of lush scented candles. If you are looking for cute kids' clothes, the brand also has a childrenswear store off Bastille.
• FrenchTrotters, 128 rue Vieille du Temple, 3rd arr., frenchtrotters.fr

Not Just Another Place

Questioned about the concept behind his beloved neighbourhood wine bar and restaurant, Chef Romain Tischenko states that it's "pour donner à boire et à manger". Just a place to grab a drink and some food. But not any place. The three-square-metre kitchen sees things like black angus marrying anchovies, or chocolate ganache linking up with olive oil. All the matches are made in heaven, as are the natural wines meant to go along with them.
• Cave à Michel, 36 Rue Saint-Marthe

Keep it Simple

Paris is in the throes of a quiet revolution that has seen gastronomy take a turn for simpler, more honest fare. This quaint café offers a rein-vigorated take on bistro cuisine, with inspired dishes like smoked mackerel with labneh, almonds and red orach or a pine nut tart with gwell ice cream. But don't count on finding these—it's just three entrees and two mains a day, depending on the season and the chefs' mood.
• Café du Coin, 9 Rue Camille Desmoulins

Sous le Ciel de Paris

There's no sign on the door at the entrance to *Le Perchoir*, but chances are you'll spot the place from far away because of the huge line at the door. This bar and restaurant combo in Ménilmon-tant has become hugely popular—and for good reason. The view from the rooftop bar on the sev-enth floor is breathtaking. And the drink menu includes some great cocktails and beers from all over the world. If you want to avoid the line downstairs, either come fairly early or rather late. Alternatively, just book a table at the restaurant one floor down—the views are just as nice and the food won't disappoint.
• Le Perchoir, 14 Rue Crespin du Gast, 20th arr., leperchoir.fr

Culture · Food **Tender is the Day, Wild is the Night**

Located in the northeastern part of the city, the former working class neighbourhoods of Belleville and Ménilmontant are in the middle of a transition. What used to be an almost forgotten part of town is steadily becoming quite fashionable, and rightfully so—the 19th and 20th arrondissements have plenty to offer. Perched on a hill with magnificent views of the whole city, Ménilmontant was a village before it was swallowed up by the mega city that is Paris. There are a few beautiful spots here it would be a shame for any visitor to miss. Most famous of all is certainly the *Père Lachaise Cemetery*. Artists, aristocrats from centuries ago and many notable figures of Parisian public life are buried here. Among them of course is Oscar Wilde, whose grave is still covered in kisses. Plus Frédéric Chopin, Jim Morrison and the great Édith Piaf. A bit further north lies the *Parc des Buttes Chaumont* (pictured)—a recent addition to the greenery of Paris and another perfect opportunity to soak up the view. Nightlife is big in Belleville and many bars offer a great atmosphere and fairly priced drinks. *Aux Folies* is a nightlife institution always packed to the brim with locals. The terrace is crowded in both winter and summer—thanks to heating lamps and small tables. Sometimes the crowd spills out onto the tiny street next to Aux Folies and you might find yourself in the middle of a spontaneous block party. Another fixture is *La Laverie*—a neighbourhood bar that plays good music, serves charming cocktails and has a notoriously friendly staff. This place always hits the spot.

• 19th and 20th arr., various locations,

Kristen de la Vallière
She's an art director, fine art curator and design consultant. Upon
noticing the lack of recognition for
so many talented designers across
Europe, she decided to start 'say
hi to_', an online platform and
gallery that's led her around the
world again and again

Kristen de la Vallière, Design Consultant

Golden Ratio

From travelling to speak at design conferences to having special
pieces made just for 'say hi to_', the line between life and work
is a blurry one for Kristen. Here, the aesthete talks champagne,
pessimism and entrepreneurship in the City of Lights

What's your relationship with the city?

Paris is one of my great loves. It's been nourishing, challenging, dramatic, loving, inspiring, cosy and has filled me with passion. Everything a great love should be.

And what's your project's relationship to the city?

Paris gives me the inspiration, space and tempo I need to create. It has a great work and life balance and the first priority in French life is to enjoy. To slow down and enjoy gives me the energy and space to have ideas and to connect to other creatives. Paris is a bit conservative and not the most entrepreneurial of places, which means it's a great place to come not to have much competition!

Where is the best place to have a glass of champagne and watch the world go by?

Well I prefer the hidden gems where I can successfully daydream and feel away from it all so I would have to say the garden of *Hotel Particulier*, on warm spring evenings.

And where should we be spending our latest nights?

At your French lover's apartment, hopefully.

One place worth crossing town for?

To get a coffee at *10 Belles* and then crossing the canal for the best croissant from *Du Pain et des Idées*.

You travel a lot for work—what's the thing you usually find yourself missing about Paris?

I miss knowing all of the characters in my neighbourhood, the guys at the fromagerie, the vegetable market, the local *Pizza Hut*. (Yes, I am even on a first name basis with those guys—guilty pleasure!) I also just generally miss the cosiness of

the city. I miss having a glass of wine and a cigarette (without being judged) around some bread, French cheese and lots of butter with friends on a terrace and being able to daydream and still get myself home without GPS on the beautiful, windy streets. I also actually really miss speaking French most when I am away—after spending so many years learning it!

And what do you NEVER miss?

Grey skies, dog shit, the enthusiastic national pessimism.

Where have you met the most interesting people in town?

Le Pigalle Hotel has a great co-work area in the front of the restaurant downstairs. I work from there a lot and see a lot of familiar faces, meet new people and have great creative exchanges. It is a cosy, familiar and cool place to meet people easily in a city where strangers don't usually mingle.

Favorite galleries right now?

Galerie Perrotin, Galerie Thaddaeus Ropac, Galerie Derouillon.

Museums that never bore you, no matter how many times you go?

Musée Bourdelle is probably my favourite museum in Paris. It's free and it is part outdoor sculpture park, part museum and part restored atelier space of the French sculptor Antoine Bourdelle. Sometimes I go there and just lay on the bench in the park area and listen to music, smoke a cigarette and come up with ideas. Otherwise, *Fondation Jean Arp, Atelier Brancusi, Villa Savoye* and *Maison La Roche* by Le Corbusier...

Favorite places to grab drinks or a nice meal after seeing a good show?

Au Passage in Le Marais is definitely my favourite restaurant in

On the outskirts of Paris lies Villa Savoye, where Le Corbusier introduced modern architecture to the world

Paris and is right around the corner from all of my favourite galleries. It's also nice to pop by *Vivant* in the 10th to meet friends for a chic and cozy place for a glass of wine or *La Belle Epoque* near Opéra for something a bit fancy.

You can put together a team of 4 Parisians to go on a day trip outside of the city. They can be real, fictitious, alive or dead... who do you bring and where do you guys go?

Well one of them would be fashion designer Pierre Cardin because then he could invite us to his house 'Palais Bulles' designed by Antti Lovag in the South of France. I'd also like to invite Charles and Marie-Laure de Noailles who were two of 20th century France's most daring and influential art patrons. (They had a rowdy and interesting creative crew including Man Ray and Dalí who they could invite to Palais Bulles for a pool party.) I'd also bring my friend Alexandra because she's the most fun French chick I know and it would be good to know at least one person on this road trip...

If we wanted to pick up something truly beautiful and unique for our home, where would you send us?

Honestly, I would say probably *Le Bon Marché*... which is a big department store but which has an excellent furniture design selection. Otherwise to go to *Les Puces de Saint-Ouen*, which is a labyrinth of outdoor furniture markets just on the outskirts of Paris. It is magical even if you don't buy something!

Something not many people might know about Paris?

It's not a very expensive place to live although it is nearly impossible to get an apartment as a foreigner. People are really friendly, especially when you learn French. France is

a pretty hard place to own a business which means that if you have a good idea from abroad, you can probably import it here and have a successful chance at a business with little to no competition.

If you could have something designed for the city, what would it be?

A modernist apartment building which foreign entrepreneurs didn't need 6756529 papers we aren't eligible to get, to have a chance to rent a place in. Just sayin'...

Located in an 18th century mansion, Galerie Emmanuel Perrotin exhibits the big names of contemporary art

Pièce de Résistance

Sweet Teeth

Buly have mastered perfumes, candles and bodycare, and consecrated them in enchanting packaging. The most interesting are their dental opiates—flavoured with apples from Montauban and mint tea, and mixed with mineral water from a special thermal spring in Castéra-Verduzan.
• Opiat Dentaire, Buly, buly1803.com

Books

The Map and the Territory
• Michel Houellebecq, 2010

Before he was slicing up the French political establishment with "Soumission", bad boy intellectual Houellebecq was lavishing his eloquent cynicism upon the art world with this withering account of an artist's rise to stardom in Paris.

A Moveable Feast
• Ernest Hemingway, 1964

Published posthumously in 1964, this memoir documents Hemingway's time in Paris in the 1920s. Look out for stories of other literary giants from those heady days—such as Fitzgerald and Stein—and tender memories of his first wife Hadley.

Suite Française
• Irène Némirovsky, 1942/2004

These first two books of an intended five-part series depict life during the Nazi occupation of France—and, unusually, were written at the time. Némirovsky was murdered in Auschwitz and her daughter discovered her manuscript half a century later.

Movies

Last Tango In Paris
• Bernardo Bertolucci, 1972

Marlon Brando and Maria Schneider star in this film about an American widower and his affair with a young Parisian. After watching it, you'll never be able to walk on the Pont Bir-Hakeim, just underneath the Passy métro, without hearing Gato Barbieri's lascivious trumpet in your head.

Paris Je T'aime
• Various, 2006

This compilation of 18 short films portraying almost all corners of the city represents a cinematic love letter to Paris. There are funny moments, tragic love stories, secret romances—and even vampires. Directors include Joel and Ethan Cohen, Gus van Sant and Alfonso Cuarón.

Bande à Part
• Jean-Luc Godard, 1964

In his seminal work the new wave auteur has Anna Karina, flanked by Sami Frey and Claude Brasseur, race against time to beat the world record for running through the Louvre galleries. That scene alone makes it worth watching this classic.

Music

I Love Paris
• Screamin' Jay Hawkins, 1958

There are countless versions of Cole Porter's ode to Paris—among them, interpretations by Ella Fitzgerald and Frank Sinatra. But when you hear Hawkins putting his unmistakable twist on this classic, you realise you're listening to something special.

La Chanson de Prévert
• Serge Gainsbourg, 1961

The legendary lover is a staple on any Paris playlist. This sentimental tale about love, loss and music that brings back memories is one of the big ballads on his third album L'Étonnant Serge Gainsbourg. As in his earlier songs, he's backed by the great Alain Goraguer Orchestra.

Life Goes On If You Are Lucky
• Nico Motte, 2015

Paris-based Nico Motte is a graphic designer by trade—and his understanding of visual space translates perfectly into the sonic medium. This EP is full of rising synths and sparse techno references, a swirling journey through tranquility and velocity. A solid instrumental to back contemplation through transport.

Back
in '82

Back in '82

Anonymous Work

I forget how the idea of selling acid at Jim Morrison's grave first occurred to me, but when it did it seemed like a pretty good one. Turned out it was too—it only took about a week and a half hanging out in Père Lachaise to finance my next three months in Europe. I bought two sheets of blotter on Telegraph and mailed it to a friend in Paris accordionned inside a cassette. It was decent, garden variety blotter, and I called it "Electric Warrior" because of the T-Rex cassette I sent it in. Between the market forces of supply, demand, and relative strengths of the franc, dollar and various kroner at the time, I was able to pull in close to a thousand percent profit and still be offering a good deal to the stream of quiet Scandinavians who flowed through to pay their respects to the Lizard King. When they'd ask "Where's it from?" I'd say "Berkeley"and their eyes would go wide and they'd repeat the word "Berkeley" like it was Xanadu.

So anyway, it was something like my third day on the job and along with the Norwegians, Danes and Swedes there's this quiet Russian dude with a guitar, Vladimir, who's there to pay his respects like the rest of us. Although he wasn't interested in my product, when he found out I was from San Francisco he got really animated and wanted to hear every- thing I could tell him about it—the music especially. I guess like a lot of people he thought it was just 1967 forever by the bay with the Airplane and the Dead still playing in the park... I told him about the handful of Dead shows I'd seen, and he got a far off look and said "Just to see Jerry... Y'know? Just to be there and see his fingers and lips moving and hear the music at the same time... Man..." he sighed. "Hey now," I said, "it'll hap- pen." He just shook his head in that way people do when there's just too much to explain. Vlad was like that a lot.

Lots of people bring their guitars to Jim's grave, thinking they're going to play something. But when they get there they seem to understand pretty quickly it's not right. Vlad though, he just sat down next to the grave, pulled his guitar out of its case and did "Crystal Ship" while the rest of us just sat there stunned. It was like Jim's voice coming up out of the ground and straight out of this guy's mouth. Like Mr. Mojo himself risin' up from the grave.

His case had the tell-tale bills and coins of a busker, and when a couple of Swedes started towards it with some francs he politely waved them off. He was off work, he said. Likewise when he finished and we asked him to do more. He just smiled politely, sweetly even, and begged off. He said we could see him at the Metro station at Les Halles if we wanted to: he was there every day. I gotta say, the guy had class. And a lot of what Hemingway called "the dignity of an iceberg..." that quiet aura about him that let you know you were seeing only a fraction of what was beneath the surface. The next day I figured what the hell, went down to Les Halles and watched him do a couple of sets. Mostly old stuff: Leonard Cohen, Jacques Brel, some Neil, of course. His mainstay though, believe it or not, was Donovan. Back then he had the look, or at least the hair. But he also had that far-off quality, that sort of otherworldliness that Donovan had. He was pretty solid through and through, but there were some songs... man. His "Let it Be" came with a sort of emotion that was practically transcendent.

We talked for a bit between songs. He was staying at a hostel and I told him he was welcome to crash at my place for awhile. The guy I was staying with was in Morocco for a couple of weeks, so I had a place all to myself in Saint-Denis. I made the offer without hesitation, there was something about him that let me know immediately that I could trust him. But there was something else too—that hint of something buried deep inside him that cried out for help, or at the very least just needed a friend.

They say that youth is wasted on the young, and I suppose most of the time that's true. But there are times in youth that aren't wasted at all, when you're young and free and friends and lovers are all plentiful and beautiful and smart and funny... you're living the life and you know it. Every relationship, even every conversation, is meaningful and beautiful somehow, no matter how brief. Those weeks with Vlad and the neighbour girls in Saint-Denis were like that.

I'll never forget how he put it, he said "You know how you hippies in America, when you talk about authorities you talk about 'the man...' Well in Russia, that is me. I am that man."

We were drinking wine and playing chess, Babette and Lisbeth dutifully writing in their journals. We all kept journals back then. Anyway, Vlad had been pressing me for details on a Hot Tuna show I saw at the Sweetwater when Grace came in and did a couple of songs. "Wooden Ships," was the only one I really remembered... (fucking mushrooms— so tough to get the dosage right.) He had a real thing for Grace Slick and hell, who could blame him? I'd told him how she dropped in at the Sweetwater all the time and made some remark about how someday we'd see her together and he went stiff. It wasn't hard to tell when something bothered Vlad, believe me: you could feel the temperature of the whole room drop. That's when he told me about being in the KGB. The rest is history.

source: Kos Media, LLC

Also available from LOST iN